Doenjang Korean Soybean Paste Recipes

Traditional and Modern Dishes Celebrating the Flavors of Doenjang

While every precaution has been taken in the preparation of this book, the publisher assumes no responsibility for errors or omissions, or for damages resulting from the use of the information contained herein.

DOENJANG KOREAN SOYBEAN PASTE RECIPES

First edition. January 22, 2024.

Copyright © 2024 john ahmad.

ISBN: 979-8224379576

Written by john ahmad.

Table of Contents

John Ahmad

Chapter 1: Introduction to Doenjang

Welcome to the enchanting world of doenjang! In this chapter, I invite you to join me on a captivating journey into the heart of Korean cuisine, where the star of the show is none other than doenjang—the savory and aromatic soybean paste that has been cherished for centuries.

As you embark on this culinary adventure, we will explore the origins of doenjang, tracing its roots back to ancient Korea and its influences from Chinese fermented bean pastes. You'll gain a deeper understanding of the intricate art of fermentation, which plays a vital role in the creation of doenjang and is a cornerstone of Korean culinary traditions.

Prepare to discover how doenjang holds a significant place in Korean households, where it is revered as a key ingredient in a wide array of dishes. We'll dive into its diverse regional variations and the fascinating ways in which it is incorporated into traditional recipes, infusing them with depth, complexity, and an explosion of flavors.

One of the most remarkable aspects of doenjang is its remarkable flavor profile and captivating aroma. I will guide you through an exploration of its distinctive taste, which can only be described as a harmonious balance of umami-rich goodness. The secret behind its allure lies in the fermentation process, which imparts deep and complex flavors that enhance every dish fortunate enough to be graced by its presence.

Beyond its incredible taste, doenjang also offers a host of nutritional benefits. We will uncover the healthful qualities of doenjang, including its high protein content and essential nutrients, making it a nourishing addition to your culinary repertoire.

In our quest to understand and appreciate doenjang fully, we will explore the various types and varieties available. From the traditional homemade doenjang, crafted with time-honored methods and aged to perfection, to the modern adaptations found in commercial brands, you'll discover a diverse range of options to suit your taste and cooking preferences.

So, join me as we embark on this captivating journey into the world of doenjang. Open your senses to the wonders of this beloved Korean soybean paste and prepare to be inspired by its rich history, complex flavors, and the myriad of possibilities it presents in the kitchen. Get ready to elevate your culinary creations with the enchanting magic of doenjang.

Chapter 2: The History and Significance of Doenjang in Korean Cuisine

Welcome to the fascinating world of doenjang and its remarkable journey through Korean history! In this chapter, we will delve into the captivating tale of doenjang, tracing its origins, understanding its cultural significance, and exploring its deep-rooted connection to Korean cuisine.

Let's travel back in time to ancient Korea, where the story of doenjang begins. Centuries ago, our ancestors discovered the magic of fermented soybean products, setting the stage for the creation of this beloved paste. As trade and cultural exchanges flourished, Chinese fermented bean pastes influenced Korean cuisine, introducing new techniques and flavors that would shape the development of doenjang.

As centuries passed, doenjang transitioned from being a humble ingredient to becoming an essential part of Korean households. It became a culinary staple, finding its place in everyday meals as well as special occasions. Doenjang's versatility and incredible taste became woven into the fabric of Korean identity, symbolizing the rich and diverse culinary heritage of the nation.

Within families, the art of making doenjang was passed down through generations, with each household having its unique recipes and secret ingredients. These traditional methods and family recipes infused doenjang with a sense of nostalgia, connecting people to their roots and preserving a treasured cultural practice.

Over time, doenjang has evolved to meet the changing tastes and preferences of modern society. It has adapted to fusion cuisine, embracing innovative culinary approaches and finding its way into international dishes. Yet, amidst this evolution, doenjang remains a symbol of tradition and an essential part of the Korean food revolution, which has seen a resurgence of interest in authentic Korean flavors and ingredients.

Beyond its significance in the culinary realm, doenjang has also made its mark in art and literature, serving as a source of inspiration and cultural references. Paintings, poems, and stories have depicted the allure and symbolism of doenjang, capturing the essence of Korean culture and identity.

In recent years, as Korean cuisine has gained global recognition, doenjang has emerged as a cultural ambassador, representing the depth and complexity of Korean flavors. It has become a cherished ingredient not only within Korea but also among food enthusiasts worldwide, elevating dishes and providing a unique taste experience.

Preserving the legacy of doenjang is of utmost importance. Dedicated efforts have been made to protect and promote traditional doenjang production methods, ensuring that the art and craftsmanship behind this remarkable paste are safeguarded for future generations. Cultural organizations and initiatives play a vital role in supporting the heritage of doenjang, aiming to maintain its authenticity and celebrate its cultural significance.

So, dear readers, immerse yourself in the captivating history of doenjang, for within its story lies a deeper understanding of Korean culinary traditions and cultural identity. Let the legacy of doenjang inspire you as you embark on your culinary journey, exploring the multitude of flavors and possibilities that this beloved soybean paste offers.

Chapter 3: Essential Ingredients for Doenjang-Based Recipes

Welcome to the heart and soul of doenjang-based recipes! In this chapter, we will explore the essential ingredients that lay the foundation for creating mouthwatering dishes infused with the rich flavors of doenjang. By understanding these key components, you'll be able to craft authentic and delicious creations that showcase the true essence of Korean cuisine.

Let's dive right into the essential ingredients that make doenjang shine:

Soybeans: At the core of doenjang lies the humble soybean. These legumes are the primary ingredient in doenjang production, lending their nutty and savory characteristics to the final product. When selecting soybeans, aim for high-quality ones that will impart the best flavor and texture to your doenjang.

Fermentation Agents: Meju and Jangdok: To transform soybeans into doenjang, fermentation agents play a crucial role. Meju, a solid fermented soybean brick, serves as the foundation for doenjang. Jangdok, the fermentation vessel, contributes to the complexity and depth of flavor during the fermentation process.

Salt: A key component in doenjang fermentation, salt not only balances flavors but also acts as a natural preservative. Choosing the right type and quality of salt is essential to achieving the desired taste and texture in your doenjang.

Rice Powder: Adding depth to the fermentation process, rice powder enriches the flavors and helps create a desirable consistency in doenjang.

Preparing rice powder and incorporating it into the fermentation process is crucial for achieving the desired results.

Water: The elixir of fermentation, water quality plays a significant role in doenjang production. The choice of water and its properties can influence the overall flavor profile and fermentation process of your doenjang.

Aromatics and Seasonings: Infusing Flavor: Garlic, ginger, and other aromatics are often used to enhance the depth of flavor in doenjang-based dishes. Traditional seasonings, such as soy sauce or fish sauce, complement the umami notes of doenjang, creating a harmonious blend of flavors.

Vegetables and Herbs: Adding Freshness and Texture: Incorporating fresh vegetables and herbs can bring brightness, texture, and additional nutritional value to your doenjang-based recipes. Experimenting with a variety of vegetables and herbs allows you to tailor the flavor profile to your preferences.

Chili Pepper: Spicy Variations with Gochujang: For those who enjoy a bit of heat, gochujang, a fermented chili pepper paste, can be combined with doenjang to add a delightful kick and complexity to your dishes.

Sweeteners: Balancing Umami and Sweetness: Sugar, honey, and other sweeteners can be used to balance the umami flavors of doenjang with a touch of sweetness. Achieving the right balance is key to creating a harmonious taste experience.

Optional Ingredients: Customizing Your Doenjang Creations: Feel free to unleash your creativity and experiment with optional ingredients to add your own personal touch to doenjang-based recipes. From spices and herbs to unique additions, the possibilities are endless when it comes to customizing your culinary creations.

By familiarizing yourself with these essential ingredients, you'll have the tools to unlock the full potential of doenjang in your cooking. So let's embrace the magic of soybeans, fermentation agents, salt, rice powder, water, aromatics, seasonings, vegetables, herbs, chili pepper, sweeteners, and optional ingredients, as we embark on a culinary adventure that celebrates the exquisite flavors of doenjang in every dish we create.

Chapter 4: Homemade Doenjang: A Step-by-Step Guide

Welcome to the exciting world of homemade doenjang! In this chapter, I will guide you through the process of creating your very own batch of authentic and delicious doenjang in the comfort of your own kitchen. Get ready to embark on a culinary adventure as we dive into the step-by-step guide to making homemade doenjang.

Understanding the Art of Homemade Doenjang

Making doenjang from scratch allows you to connect with tradition, embrace the satisfaction of creating something with your own hands, and customize the flavors to your liking. It's an art form that has been passed down through generations, and now you can master it.

Gathering the Ingredients

To make homemade doenjang, you will need:

- 2 cups dried soybeans
- 2 tablespoons doenjang starter culture (or 1 cup crumbled meju)
- 1 cup coarse sea salt
- Optional ingredients for customization (such as garlic, ginger, or chili flakes)
- Preparing the Soybeans

Follow these steps to prepare the soybeans:

1. Rinse the dried soybeans under cold water and remove any debris.
2. Soak the soybeans in water overnight or for at least 8 hours.
3. Drain the soybeans and transfer them to a large pot.

4. Add enough water to cover the soybeans and bring to a boil.
5. Reduce the heat and simmer for 2 to 3 hours until the soybeans are soft and easily mashed.

Fermentation Agents: Meju

Meju is the fermented soybean brick that serves as the base for doenjang. Here's how you can make meju:

1. Take the cooked soybeans and mash them into a paste-like consistency.
2. Shape the soybean paste into rectangular blocks or small patties.
3. Place the meju in a warm and well-ventilated area to ferment for 2 to 3 days until the surface develops a white mold.

Jang Dok: The Fermentation Vessel

Select a suitable jangdok vessel for fermenting the meju and creating doenjang. You can use a traditional onggi earthenware jar or a glass container with an airtight lid.

The Fermentation Process

Once you have your meju and jangdok ready, it's time to start the fermentation process:

1. Crumble the meju into small pieces and place them into the jangdok vessel.
2. Add the coarse sea salt, mixing it thoroughly with the meju.
3. Cover the vessel with a clean cloth or lid, leaving a small opening for air circulation.
4. Store the jangdok in a cool, dark place with a temperature around 55-65°F (13-18°C) for 6 to 12 months.
5. Aging and Maturing Doenjang

As time passes, your doenjang will continue to develop its flavors. Here's what you need to do during the aging process:

1. Periodically check on the doenjang, removing any mold that forms on the surface.
2. Stir the doenjang gently every few weeks to promote even fermentation.
3. Taste the doenjang periodically to assess its flavor development. It should have a deep, rich, and savory taste when it's ready.
4. Testing for Readiness

To determine if your homemade doenjang is ready for consumption, consider the following factors:

1. Aroma: It should have a distinct, savory aroma with notes of fermentation.
2. Taste: The flavor should be robust, complex, and well-balanced.
3. Texture: It should have a smooth consistency, similar to a thick paste.

Storing and Preserving Homemade Doenjang

Once your homemade doenjang is ready, store it properly to maintain its quality:

1. Transfer the doenjang to a clean jar or container with an airtight lid.
2. Keep it in the refrigerator to slow down the fermentation process and maintain its flavor and freshness.
3. Homemade doenjang can be stored for several months to a year, becoming more flavorful over time.

Cooking with Homemade Doenjang

Your homemade doenjang is now ready to be used in a variety of delicious recipes. Here are some traditional and creative ideas to get you started:

1. Doenjang Jjigae: A classic doenjang stew with tofu, vegetables, and protein of your choice.
2. Doenjang Gui: Marinate your favorite meats or vegetables with doenjang for a flavorful grilled dish.
3. Doenjang Bibimbap: A vibrant and nutritious rice bowl topped with an array of vegetables and a dollop of doenjang.

Enjoy the fruits of your labor as you savor the authentic flavors of your homemade doenjang. From the initial preparation of the soybeans to the fermentation and aging process, you have embarked on a culinary journey that connects you to Korean tradition. Let your homemade doenjang elevate your dishes and bring the rich and complex taste of Korean cuisine into your home.

Chapter 5: Classic Doenjang Recipes

In this chapter, we will explore three classic doenjang recipes that have been cherished in Korean cuisine for generations. These dishes showcase the versatility and depth of flavor that doenjang brings to the table. Get ready to immerse yourself in the rich and comforting world of doenjang with Doenjang Jjigae, Doenjang Guk, and Doenjang Samgyeopsal.

a. Doenjang Jjigae (Doenjang Stew)

Doenjang Jjigae is a hearty and satisfying stew that is beloved in Korean households. Its robust flavors and comforting warmth make it a perfect dish for any time of the year. Here's how you can make this classic recipe:

Ingredients:

- 1 tablespoon sesame oil
- 1 onion, thinly sliced
- 2 cloves of garlic, minced
- 1 zucchini, sliced
- 1 potato, peeled and cubed
- 1 cup tofu, cubed
- 2 tablespoons doenjang (Korean soybean paste)
- 4 cups vegetable or anchovy broth
- Optional: 1 green chili pepper, sliced

Instructions:

1. Heat sesame oil in a pot over medium heat. Add the onion and garlic, and sauté until they become fragrant and slightly

softened.

2. Add zucchini and potato to the pot, and continue to cook for a few minutes until they start to soften.
3. Stir in the tofu cubes and doenjang, mixing well to coat the ingredients.
4. Pour in the vegetable or anchovy broth, and bring the mixture to a boil.
5. Reduce the heat to a simmer and let the stew cook for about 15-20 minutes, until the vegetables are tender and the flavors have melded together.
6. If desired, add the sliced green chili pepper for an extra kick of spiciness.
7. Serve hot with a bowl of steamed rice for a comforting and flavorful meal.

b. Doenjang Guk (Doenjang Soup)

Doenjang Guk is a simple yet nourishing soup that is often enjoyed as part of a traditional Korean meal. Its light and delicate flavors make it an excellent choice for a comforting appetizer or a light lunch. Here's how you can prepare this soothing soup:

Ingredients:

- 4 cups water
- 2 tablespoons doenjang (Korean soybean paste)
- 1 tablespoon dried anchovies or kelp (optional, for broth)
- 2 green onions, thinly sliced
- 1 cup sliced mushrooms (such as shiitake or button mushrooms)
- 1/2 cup sliced zucchini
- 1/2 cup sliced tofu
- Optional: 1 teaspoon sesame oil

Instructions:

1. If using dried anchovies or kelp, simmer them in water for 10-15 minutes to create a flavorful broth. Strain the broth, discarding the anchovies or kelp.
2. In a pot, bring the broth (or water) to a gentle boil.
3. Dilute the doenjang in a small amount of water to make a smooth paste.
4. Add the diluted doenjang to the boiling broth, stirring well to incorporate it into the liquid.
5. Add the green onions, mushrooms, zucchini, and tofu to the pot.
6. Simmer the soup over medium heat for about 10 minutes until the vegetables are tender and the flavors have melded together.
7. If desired, drizzle sesame oil over the soup before serving for added aroma and richness.
8. Ladle the hot Doenjang Guk into bowls and enjoy its comforting flavors.

These recipes are just the beginning of the culinary possibilities that await you on your journey with doenjang. So gather your ingredients, fire up the stove or grill, and savor the authentic tastes of these beloved Korean dishes.

Chapter 6: Doenjang Side Dishes

In this chapter, we will explore three delightful side dishes that feature the incredible flavors of doenjang. These dishes are perfect for adding a burst of savory goodness to your meals. Get ready to enhance your dining experience with Kongnamul Muchim, Oi Doenjang Muchim, and Gamja Doenjang Bokkeum.

a. Kongnamul Muchim (Seasoned Soybean Sprouts)

Kongnamul Muchim is a refreshing and nutritious side dish that pairs perfectly with any Korean meal. The combination of crunchy soybean sprouts and the umami taste of doenjang creates a harmonious blend of flavors. Here's how you can make this simple yet delicious side dish:

Ingredients:

- 2 cups soybean sprouts
- 1 tablespoon doenjang (Korean soybean paste)
- 1 teaspoon soy sauce
- 1 teaspoon sesame oil
- 1 clove of garlic, minced
- Optional: Sliced green onions and sesame seeds for garnish

Instructions:

1. Rinse the soybean sprouts under cold water to remove any impurities.
2. Bring a pot of water to a boil and blanch the soybean sprouts for

about 1-2 minutes until they are slightly tender.

3. Drain the sprouts and rinse them with cold water to stop the cooking process. Allow them to cool completely.
4. In a bowl, combine doenjang, soy sauce, sesame oil, and minced garlic to make the dressing.
5. Add the cooled soybean sprouts to the bowl and toss them with the dressing until they are well coated.
6. Garnish with sliced green onions and sesame seeds, if desired.
7. Serve the Kongnamul Muchim chilled as a refreshing side dish that complements the main course beautifully.

b. Oi Doenjang Muchim (Cucumber Doenjang Salad)

Oi Doenjang Muchim is a light and tangy cucumber salad infused with the savory flavors of doenjang. This side dish provides a cool and crisp contrast to rich and bold main dishes. Here's how you can prepare this refreshing salad:

Ingredients:

- 1 English cucumber, thinly sliced
- 1 tablespoon doenjang (Korean soybean paste)
- 1 tablespoon rice vinegar
- 1 teaspoon sesame oil
- 1 teaspoon honey or sugar
- Optional: Thinly sliced red chili pepper for a spicy kick

Instructions:

1. In a bowl, combine doenjang, rice vinegar, sesame oil, and honey (or sugar) to create the dressing.
2. Add the thinly sliced cucumber to the bowl and toss it with the dressing until the cucumber slices are well coated.
3. If desired, add thinly sliced red chili pepper for a spicy variation.
4. Allow the flavors to meld together by refrigerating the salad for

at least 15 minutes before serving.

5. Serve the Oi Doenjang Muchim as a refreshing and zesty side dish alongside your main course.

c. Gamja Doenjang Bokkeum (Stir-Fried Potatoes with Doenjang)

Gamja Doenjang Bokkeum showcases the versatility of doenjang by adding depth and flavor to stir-fried potatoes. This side dish is hearty, satisfying, and pairs well with rice or as a banchan (side dish) in a Korean meal. Here's how you can create this delicious stir-fry:

Ingredients:

- 2 medium-sized potatoes, peeled and cut into bite-sized pieces
- 1 tablespoon doenjang (Korean soybean paste)
- 1 tablespoon soy sauce
- 1 teaspoon honey or sugar
- 1 tablespoon vegetable oil
- Optional: Thinly sliced green onions for garnish

Instructions:

1. Heat vegetable oil in a pan or wok over medium heat.
2. Add the potato pieces to the pan and stir-fry them until they start to turn golden brown and are cooked through.
3. In a small bowl, mix doenjang, soy sauce, and honey (or sugar) to make the seasoning sauce.
4. Pour the seasoning sauce over the cooked potatoes and stir-fry for an additional 2-3 minutes, ensuring that the potatoes are evenly coated.
5. If desired, garnish with thinly sliced green onions for added freshness and aroma.
6. Serve the Gamja Doenjang Bokkeum hot as a flavorful and

comforting side dish.

Enjoy the delightful flavors of Kongnamul Muchim, Oi Doenjang Muchim, and Gamja Doenjang Bokkeum as they complement your main course and bring a burst of savory goodness to your table. These side dishes are versatile and can be enjoyed as part of a Korean meal or alongside dishes from various cuisines. So, bring the vibrant tastes of doenjang into your culinary repertoire and elevate your dining experience.

Chapter 7: Doenjang and Noodles

In this chapter, we will explore the wonderful combination of doenjang and noodles. Whether you're craving a comforting bowl of broth-based noodles or a spicy noodle dish, these recipes featuring doenjang will satisfy your cravings. Get ready to indulge in Janchi Guksu, Bibim Guksu, and Doenjang Ramyeon.

a. Janchi Guksu (Korean Banquet Noodles with Doenjang Broth)

Janchi Guksu is a traditional Korean dish consisting of thin wheat noodles served in a flavorful broth. The addition of doenjang elevates this dish with its umami-rich taste. Here's how you can make this comforting and satisfying noodle dish:

Ingredients:

- 8 ounces dried wheat noodles (somyeon or thin udon noodles)
- 4 cups vegetable or chicken broth
- 2 tablespoons doenjang (Korean soybean paste)
- 1 tablespoon soy sauce
- 1 teaspoon sesame oil
- Sliced green onions and julienned cucumber for garnish
- Optional: Hard-boiled eggs, shredded chicken, or sliced beef for added protein

Instructions:

1. Cook the noodles according to the package instructions until they are al dente. Drain and rinse them under cold water to remove excess starch. Set aside.

2. In a pot, bring the vegetable or chicken broth to a simmer over medium heat.
3. In a small bowl, dilute the doenjang with a small amount of the hot broth to create a smooth paste.
4. Add the doenjang paste, soy sauce, and sesame oil to the pot of broth, stirring well to combine.
5. Allow the broth to simmer for 5-7 minutes to let the flavors meld together.
6. Divide the cooked noodles into individual serving bowls and ladle the hot doenjang broth over the noodles.
7. Garnish with sliced green onions, julienned cucumber, and any additional protein of your choice.
8. Serve the Janchi Guksu hot and enjoy the comforting flavors of the doenjang-infused broth.

b. Bibim Guksu (Spicy Doenjang Noodles)

Bibim Guksu is a refreshing and spicy noodle dish that features a delightful combination of flavors and textures. By incorporating doenjang into the sauce, you'll experience a savory kick that complements the vibrant ingredients. Here's how you can prepare this zesty and satisfying noodle dish:

Ingredients:

- 8 ounces dried somyeon (thin wheat) noodles or soba noodles
- 2 tablespoons doenjang (Korean soybean paste)
- 1 tablespoon gochujang (Korean chili paste)
- 1 tablespoon rice vinegar
- 1 tablespoon sesame oil
- 1 teaspoon honey or sugar
- 1 clove of garlic, minced
- Sliced cucumber, julienned carrots, and bean sprouts for topping
- Optional: Thinly sliced beef or tofu for added protein

Instructions:

1. Cook the noodles according to the package instructions until they are al dente. Drain and rinse them under cold water to remove excess starch. Set aside.
2. In a bowl, combine doenjang, gochujang, rice vinegar, sesame oil, honey (or sugar), and minced garlic to create the sauce.
3. Adjust the seasoning to your taste preferences, adding more gochujang for spiciness or honey for sweetness.
4. Toss the cooked noodles with the sauce until they are evenly coated.
5. Top the noodles with sliced cucumber, julienned carrots, bean sprouts, and any additional protein of your choice.
6. Mix everything together well, ensuring that the sauce and

toppings are evenly distributed.

7. Serve the Bibim Guksu chilled or at room temperature for a refreshing and fiery noodle dish.

c. Doenjang Ramyeon (Doenjang Instant Noodles)

If you're looking for a quick and easy noodle fix with a Korean twist, Doenjang Ramyeon is the perfect choice. By incorporating doenjang into instant noodles, you'll create a flavorful and satisfying meal in no time. Here's how you can enjoy Doenjang Ramyeon:

Ingredients:

- 1 packet of instant ramyeon noodles (any flavor of your choice)
- 1 tablespoon doenjang (Korean soybean paste)
- Sliced green onions and kimchi for garnish
- Optional: Soft-boiled egg, sliced tofu, or leftover cooked meat for added protein

Instructions:

1. Cook the instant ramyeon noodles according to the package instructions.
2. While the noodles are cooking, dilute the doenjang with a small amount of hot water to create a smooth paste.
3. Once the noodles are cooked, drain them and return them to the pot.
4. Add the diluted doenjang to the pot of noodles, stirring well to evenly distribute the paste.
5. Adjust the seasoning to your taste preferences, adding more doenjang for a stronger flavor.
6. Garnish with sliced green onions, kimchi, and any additional protein of your choice.
7. Serve the Doenjang Ramyeon hot for a quick and satisfying meal.

Enjoy the delicious flavors of Janchi Guksu, Bibim Guksu, and Doenjang Ramyeon as you indulge in the savory combination of doenjang and noodles. These recipes offer a range of tastes and textures, from comforting broths to zesty sauces, allowing you to explore the versatility of doenjang in noodle dishes. So grab your favorite noodles, unleash your culinary creativity, and savor the delightful fusion of flavors in these delicious recipes.

Chapter 8: Doenjang in Marinades and Glazes

In this chapter, we will delve into the world of marinades and glazes featuring the delectable flavor of doenjang. Whether you're grilling beef, chicken wings, or tofu, incorporating doenjang will add a savory and umami-rich element to your dishes. Get ready to elevate your meals with Doenjang Bulgogi, Doenjang Chicken Wings, and Doenjang Glazed Tofu.

a. Doenjang Bulgogi (Marinated Grilled Beef)

Doenjang Bulgogi is a variation of the classic Korean bulgogi that features the deep and complex flavors of doenjang. The combination of savory marinade and smoky grilled beef creates a mouthwatering dish. Here's how you can prepare this delicious marinated grilled beef:

Ingredients:

- 1 pound beef (ribeye, sirloin, or tenderloin), thinly sliced
- 3 tablespoons doenjang (Korean soybean paste)
- 2 tablespoons soy sauce
- 2 tablespoons honey or brown sugar
- 2 cloves of garlic, minced
- 1 tablespoon sesame oil
- Optional: Thinly sliced green onions and toasted sesame seeds for garnish

Instructions:

1. In a bowl, combine doenjang, soy sauce, honey (or brown sugar), minced garlic, and sesame oil to create the marinade.

2. Add the thinly sliced beef to the marinade, ensuring that each piece is well coated. Allow it to marinate for at least 1 hour, or up to overnight in the refrigerator for more intense flavors.
3. Preheat a grill or grill pan over medium-high heat.
4. Grill the marinated beef slices for a few minutes on each side until they are cooked to your desired level of doneness.
5. Remove the grilled beef from the heat and garnish with thinly sliced green onions and toasted sesame seeds, if desired.
6. Serve the Doenjang Bulgogi with steamed rice and a side of fresh lettuce leaves for wrapping, along with other banchan (side dishes) for a complete Korean meal.

b. Doenjang Chicken Wings

Doenjang Chicken Wings are a finger-licking delight that combines the succulent flavors of chicken wings with the savory punch of doenjang. These wings are perfect for parties or as an appetizer that will leave your guests craving for more. Here's how you can prepare this irresistible dish:

Ingredients:

- 2 pounds chicken wings
- 3 tablespoons doenjang (Korean soybean paste)
- 2 tablespoons soy sauce
- 2 tablespoons honey or maple syrup
- 1 tablespoon rice vinegar
- 1 tablespoon sesame oil
- 2 cloves of garlic, minced
- Optional: Thinly sliced green onions and sesame seeds for garnish

Instructions:

1. In a bowl, combine doenjang, soy sauce, honey (or maple

syrup), rice vinegar, sesame oil, and minced garlic to create the marinade.

2. Add the chicken wings to the marinade, ensuring that each wing is well coated. Let them marinate for at least 1 hour, or up to overnight in the refrigerator for more intense flavors.

3. Preheat the oven to 400°F (200°C) and line a baking sheet with parchment paper.

4. Place the marinated chicken wings on the prepared baking sheet, ensuring they are spaced apart.

5. Bake the chicken wings for approximately 25-30 minutes, or until they are cooked through and golden brown, flipping them halfway through.

6. Remove the chicken wings from the oven and garnish with thinly sliced green onions and sesame seeds, if desired.

7. Serve the Doenjang Chicken Wings as an appetizer or main dish, accompanied by your favorite dipping sauce or as part of a Korean-inspired spread.

c. Doenjang Glazed Tofu

Doenjang Glazed Tofu is a vegetarian-friendly dish that combines the smooth texture of tofu with the savory depth of doenjang. This recipe offers a delightful contrast of flavors and can be enjoyed as a main course or a side dish. Here's how you can prepare this flavorful glazed tofu:

Ingredients:

- 1 package firm tofu, drained and cut into cubes or rectangular slices
- 2 tablespoons doenjang (Korean soybean paste)
- 2 tablespoons soy sauce
- 1 tablespoon honey or brown sugar
- 1 tablespoon sesame oil
- 1 clove of garlic, minced
- Optional: Sliced green onions and sesame seeds for garnish

Instructions:

1. In a bowl, combine doenjang, soy sauce, honey (or brown sugar), sesame oil, and minced garlic to create the glaze.
2. Place the tofu cubes or slices in a shallow dish and pour the glaze over them, ensuring that each piece is well coated. Allow them to marinate for at least 30 minutes.
3. Preheat a non-stick skillet or grill pan over medium heat.
4. Cook the marinated tofu pieces for a few minutes on each side until they are heated through and develop a slightly caramelized exterior.
5. Remove the glazed tofu from the heat and garnish with sliced green onions and sesame seeds, if desired.
6. Serve the Doenjang Glazed Tofu as a main course with steamed rice and a side of sautéed vegetables, or as a side dish alongside other Korean-inspired dishes.

Enjoy the delectable flavors of Doenjang Bulgogi, Doenjang Chicken Wings, and Doenjang Glazed Tofu as you savor the savory and rich combination of doenjang in marinades and glazes. These recipes offer a range of options, from grilled meats to vegetarian-friendly choices, allowing you to explore the versatility of doenjang in creating irresistible and flavorful dishes. So, fire up the grill or heat up the skillet, and get ready to indulge in the mouthwatering flavors of these marinated and glazed creations.

Chapter 9: Doenjang Fusion Cuisine

In this chapter, we will embark on a culinary adventure by infusing doenjang into various fusion dishes. From fried rice to pizza and pasta, these recipes combine the rich flavors of doenjang with international culinary influences. Get ready to explore the exciting world of Doenjang Fried Rice, Doenjang Pizza, and Doenjang Pasta.

a. Doenjang Fried Rice

Doenjang Fried Rice is a delicious fusion of Korean and Asian flavors, where the umami taste of doenjang adds depth to the classic fried rice. This dish is versatile, allowing you to incorporate your favorite ingredients. Here's how you can prepare this flavorful fusion dish:

Ingredients:

- 3 cups cooked rice (preferably day-old rice)
- 2 tablespoons doenjang (Korean soybean paste)
- 1 tablespoon soy sauce
- 2 cloves of garlic, minced
- 1 cup mixed vegetables (such as peas, carrots, corn, and bell peppers)
- 1 cup protein of your choice (diced chicken, shrimp, or tofu)
- 2 eggs, beaten
- 2 green onions, thinly sliced
- 1 tablespoon vegetable oil
- Optional: Sesame oil and sesame seeds for garnish

Instructions:

1. Heat vegetable oil in a large skillet or wok over medium heat.
2. Add the minced garlic and sauté until fragrant.
3. Add the mixed vegetables and protein of your choice to the skillet, and stir-fry until the vegetables are tender and the protein is cooked through.
4. Push the vegetables and protein to one side of the skillet, and pour the beaten eggs into the other side. Scramble the eggs until they are fully cooked.
5. Add the cooked rice to the skillet, breaking up any clumps with a spatula.
6. In a small bowl, mix together the doenjang and soy sauce. Pour the mixture over the rice and stir-fry everything together, ensuring that the doenjang coats the rice evenly.
7. Continue to stir-fry for a few more minutes until the rice is heated through and well combined with the vegetables, protein, and doenjang mixture.
8. Garnish with sliced green onions and, if desired, drizzle a small amount of sesame oil and sprinkle sesame seeds over the fried rice.
9. Serve the Doenjang Fried Rice hot as a satisfying and flavorful fusion dish.

b. Doenjang Pizza

Doenjang Pizza brings together the beloved Korean ingredient with the popular Italian dish, creating a unique and delicious fusion experience. The combination of savory doenjang, melted cheese, and a variety of toppings will tantalize your taste buds. Here's how you can prepare this exciting fusion pizza:

Ingredients:

- 1 pizza dough (store-bought or homemade)
- 2 tablespoons doenjang (Korean soybean paste)
- 1 cup shredded mozzarella cheese
- 1/2 cup sliced bell peppers
- 1/2 cup sliced mushrooms
- 1/4 cup sliced red onions
- 1/4 cup sliced black olives
- Optional: Sliced cooked chicken, bacon, or other toppings of your choice
- Fresh basil leaves for garnish

Instructions:

1. Preheat the oven to the temperature indicated on the pizza dough package or according to your homemade dough recipe.
2. Roll out the pizza dough on a lightly floured surface to your desired thickness.
3. Transfer the rolled-out dough onto a pizza stone, baking sheet, or pizza pan.
4. Spread the doenjang evenly over the surface of the dough, leaving a small border around the edges.
5. Sprinkle the shredded mozzarella cheese over the doenjang.
6. Arrange the sliced bell peppers, mushrooms, red onions, black olives, and any other toppings you prefer evenly on top of the cheese.

7. Place the pizza in the preheated oven and bake according to the dough instructions, usually around 12-15 minutes or until the cheese is melted and bubbly and the crust is golden brown.
8. Remove the pizza from the oven and garnish with fresh basil leaves.
9. Slice the Doenjang Pizza and serve it warm as an exciting fusion dish that combines the best of Korean and Italian flavors.

c. Doenjang Pasta

Doenjang Pasta is a fusion dish that merges the bold and savory flavors of doenjang with the classic Italian pasta. This unique combination creates a delightful umami-packed dish that will satisfy your cravings. Here's how you can prepare this delectable fusion pasta:

Ingredients:

- 8 ounces pasta of your choice (spaghetti, penne, or linguine)
- 2 tablespoons doenjang (Korean soybean paste)
- 1/4 cup heavy cream or coconut cream for a vegan option
- 2 tablespoons olive oil
- 2 cloves of garlic, minced
- 1/2 cup sliced mushrooms
- 1/2 cup sliced cherry tomatoes
- 1/4 cup sliced black olives
- Fresh parsley, chopped, for garnish
- Optional: Grated Parmesan cheese or nutritional yeast for topping

Instructions:

1. Cook the pasta according to the package instructions until it is al dente. Drain and set aside.
2. In a small bowl, mix together the doenjang and heavy cream (or coconut cream) until well combined.
3. Heat olive oil in a large skillet over medium heat. Add the minced garlic and sauté until fragrant.
4. Add the sliced mushrooms to the skillet and cook until they are softened and lightly browned.
5. Stir in the sliced cherry tomatoes and black olives, and cook for a few more minutes until the tomatoes start to soften.
6. Reduce the heat to low and add the doenjang and cream mixture to the skillet, stirring well to combine all the

ingredients.

7. Add the cooked pasta to the skillet and toss it with the sauce until the pasta is evenly coated.
8. Cook for an additional minute or two, allowing the flavors to meld together.
9. Remove from heat and garnish with fresh parsley. If desired, sprinkle grated Parmesan cheese or nutritional yeast over the pasta for added flavor.
10. Serve the Doenjang Pasta hot as a unique fusion dish that brings together the best of Korean and Italian cuisine.

Enjoy the exciting fusion flavors of Doenjang Fried Rice, Doenjang Pizza, and Doenjang Pasta as you explore the versatility of doenjang in different culinary contexts. These recipes showcase the creative possibilities of infusing Korean flavors into international dishes, adding a delightful twist to familiar favorites. So, let your taste buds embark on a delicious fusion journey and indulge in the harmonious blending of flavors in these delectable dishes.

Chapter 10: Doenjang and Seafood

In this chapter, we will explore the wonderful combination of doenjang with various seafood dishes. The umami-rich flavor of doenjang complements the delicate and briny taste of seafood, creating a harmonious fusion of flavors. Get ready to tantalize your taste buds with Grilled Doenjang Shrimp Skewers, Doenjang Jjigae with Clams, and Spicy Doenjang Steamed Fish.

a. Grilled Doenjang Shrimp Skewers

Grilled Doenjang Shrimp Skewers are a mouthwatering delight that combines the succulent sweetness of shrimp with the savory depth of doenjang. This dish is perfect for outdoor gatherings or as an appetizer that will impress your guests. Here's how you can prepare these flavorful skewers:

Ingredients:

- 1 pound shrimp, peeled and deveined
- 2 tablespoons doenjang (Korean soybean paste)
- 2 tablespoons soy sauce
- 1 tablespoon honey or brown sugar
- 1 tablespoon sesame oil
- 2 cloves of garlic, minced
- Optional: Sliced green onions and sesame seeds for garnish

Instructions:

1. In a bowl, combine doenjang, soy sauce, honey (or brown sugar), sesame oil, and minced garlic to create the marinade.
2. Add the peeled and deveined shrimp to the marinade, ensuring

that each shrimp is well coated. Allow them to marinate for about 15-30 minutes.

3. Preheat a grill or grill pan over medium-high heat.
4. Thread the marinated shrimp onto skewers.
5. Grill the shrimp skewers for 2-3 minutes on each side until they are cooked through and slightly charred.
6. Remove the shrimp skewers from the heat and garnish with sliced green onions and sesame seeds, if desired.
7. Serve the Grilled Doenjang Shrimp Skewers hot as a flavorful and enticing seafood appetizer.

b. Doenjang Jjigae with Clams

Doenjang Jjigae with Clams is a comforting and hearty stew that brings together the rich flavors of doenjang with the briny sweetness of clams. This dish is a popular choice in Korean cuisine and is best enjoyed with a bowl of steamed rice. Here's how you can prepare this delightful seafood stew:

Ingredients:

- 2 cups clams, rinsed and scrubbed
- 4 cups vegetable or seafood broth
- 2 tablespoons doenjang (Korean soybean paste)
- 1 tablespoon gochujang (Korean chili paste)
- 1 onion, thinly sliced
- 1 zucchini, sliced
- 1 green chili pepper, sliced (optional for added spiciness)
- 2 cloves of garlic, minced
- 1 tablespoon sesame oil
- Sliced green onions for garnish

Instructions:

In a large pot, bring the vegetable or seafood broth to a boil over medium heat.

1. Add the sliced onion, zucchini, and minced garlic to the pot and simmer for a few minutes until the vegetables start to soften.
2. In a small bowl, dilute the doenjang and gochujang with a small amount of the hot broth to create a smooth paste.
3. Add the diluted doenjang and gochujang mixture to the pot, stirring well to incorporate it into the broth.
4. Add the clams and green chili pepper (if using) to the pot and continue to simmer until the clams open up and are cooked through.
5. Drizzle sesame oil over the stew and stir gently to combine the flavors.
6. Remove from heat and garnish with sliced green onions.
7. Serve the Doenjang Jjigae with Clams hot, accompanied by steamed rice, for a comforting and satisfying seafood stew experience.

c. Spicy Doenjang Steamed Fish

Spicy Doenjang Steamed Fish is a delightful dish that showcases the delicate flavors of steamed fish enhanced with the bold and spicy kick of doenjang. This recipe highlights the harmony between the simplicity of steaming and the complex taste of doenjang. Here's how you can prepare this tantalizing seafood dish:

Ingredients:

- 1 whole fish (such as sea bass, red snapper, or trout), cleaned and scaled
- 2 tablespoons doenjang (Korean soybean paste)
- 1 tablespoon gochujang (Korean chili paste)
- 1 tablespoon soy sauce
- 1 tablespoon rice vinegar
- 1 tablespoon sesame oil
- 2 cloves of garlic, minced
- 1-inch piece of ginger, thinly sliced
- Sliced green onions and cilantro for garnish
- Optional: Sliced red chili peppers for extra spiciness

Instructions:

1. Rinse the cleaned and scaled fish under cold water and pat it dry with paper towels.
2. In a bowl, combine doenjang, gochujang, soy sauce, rice vinegar, sesame oil, minced garlic, and ginger to create the marinade.
3. Place the fish on a heatproof plate or steaming dish.
4. Rub the marinade mixture all over the fish, making sure to coat it evenly on both sides.
5. If desired, stuff the fish cavity with additional slices of ginger and garlic.
6. Prepare a steamer and bring the water to a boil. Place the plate or dish with the fish inside the steamer.

7. Steam the fish for approximately 12-15 minutes, or until it is cooked through and flakes easily with a fork.
8. Carefully remove the steamed fish from the steamer and transfer it to a serving plate.
9. Garnish with sliced green onions, cilantro, and, if desired, sliced red chili peppers for an extra kick.
10. Serve the Spicy Doenjang Steamed Fish hot as a centerpiece dish, accompanied by steamed rice and your favorite side dishes.

Enjoy the wonderful combination of doenjang and seafood with Grilled Doenjang Shrimp Skewers, Doenjang Jjigae with Clams, and Spicy Doenjang Steamed Fish. These recipes allow you to savor the natural flavors of seafood while infusing them with the unique savory taste of doenjang. So, dive into the delicious world of doenjang and seafood and treat yourself to these tantalizing dishes.

Chapter 11: Doenjang in Vegetarian and Vegan Dishes

In this chapter, we will explore the versatile use of doenjang in vegetarian and vegan dishes. These recipes showcase the rich umami flavors of doenjang combined with a variety of vegetables and plant-based ingredients. Get ready to enjoy the satisfying goodness of Doenjang Bibimbap, Doenjang Japchae, and Doenjang Tofu Stir-Fry.

a. Doenjang Bibimbap (Mixed Rice Bowl)

Doenjang Bibimbap is a vibrant and flavorful mixed rice bowl that features a variety of sautéed vegetables and a delectable doenjang sauce. This dish is customizable, allowing you to use your favorite vegetables and toppings. Here's how you can prepare this delightful vegetarian bibimbap:

Ingredients:

- 2 cups cooked rice (preferably short-grain rice)
- Assorted vegetables of your choice (such as carrots, spinach, bean sprouts, mushrooms, zucchini, and bell peppers), sliced or julienned
- 2 tablespoons doenjang (Korean soybean paste)
- 1 tablespoon gochujang (Korean chili paste)
- 1 tablespoon soy sauce
- 1 tablespoon sesame oil
- 2 cloves of garlic, minced

- Optional toppings: Fried egg, sliced tofu, or roasted seaweed
- Optional garnish: Sliced green onions and sesame seeds

Instructions:

1. Prepare the sautéed vegetables by lightly cooking each vegetable separately in a pan with a small amount of oil until they are tender yet still slightly crisp. Season each vegetable with a pinch of salt and set aside.
2. In a small bowl, mix together doenjang, gochujang, soy sauce, sesame oil, and minced garlic to create the bibimbap sauce.
3. Divide the cooked rice into serving bowls.
4. Arrange the sautéed vegetables on top of the rice, creating separate sections for each vegetable.
5. Drizzle the bibimbap sauce over the vegetables and rice.
6. If desired, add a fried egg, sliced tofu, or roasted seaweed on top.
7. Garnish with sliced green onions and sesame seeds.
8. To eat, mix all the ingredients together in the bowl, ensuring that the sauce is evenly distributed.
9. Enjoy the Doenjang Bibimbap as a nutritious and satisfying vegetarian meal.

b. Doenjang Japchae (Stir-Fried Glass Noodles with Vegetables)
Doenjang Japchae is a delightful dish that combines the chewy texture of glass noodles with a medley of colorful vegetables and the savory flavors of doenjang. This vegan-friendly dish is perfect as a main course or as a side dish in a Korean-inspired spread. Here's how you can prepare this mouthwatering japchae:

Ingredients:

- 8 ounces glass noodles (sweet potato noodles)
- Assorted vegetables of your choice (such as carrots, spinach, mushrooms, bell peppers, and onions), sliced or julienned
- 2 tablespoons doenjang (Korean soybean paste)
- 1 tablespoon soy sauce
- 1 tablespoon sesame oil
- 1 tablespoon maple syrup or brown sugar
- 2 cloves of garlic, minced
- Optional: Sliced green onions and sesame seeds for garnish

Instructions:

1. Cook the glass noodles according to the package instructions until they are al dente. Drain and rinse them under cold water to prevent sticking. Set aside.
2. In a small bowl, mix together doenjang, soy sauce, sesame oil, maple syrup (or brown sugar), and minced garlic to create the sauce.
3. Heat a large pan or wok over medium heat and add a small amount of oil.
4. Sauté the sliced or julienned vegetables in the pan until they are tender yet still slightly crisp.
5. Add the cooked glass noodles to the pan, followed by the sauce mixture.
6. Stir-fry everything together until the noodles are well coated

with the sauce and the flavors are well combined.

7. Remove from heat and garnish with sliced green onions and sesame seeds, if desired.

8. Serve the Doenjang Japchae warm or at room temperature as a delightful and flavorful vegetarian or vegan dish.

c. Doenjang Tofu Stir-Fry

Doenjang Tofu Stir-Fry is a quick and easy dish that combines the creamy texture of tofu with the savory depth of doenjang. This vegan-friendly recipe is packed with plant-based protein and a medley of colorful vegetables. Here's how you can prepare this delicious stir-fry:

Ingredients:

- 1 block firm tofu, cubed
- Assorted vegetables of your choice (such as bell peppers, broccoli, snow peas, carrots, and onions), sliced or diced
- 2 tablespoons doenjang (Korean soybean paste)
- 1 tablespoon soy sauce
- 1 tablespoon sesame oil
- 2 cloves of garlic, minced
- Optional: Sliced green onions and sesame seeds for garnish

Instructions:

1. Heat a large pan or wok over medium heat and add a small amount of oil.
2. Add the cubed tofu to the pan and cook until it is lightly browned on all sides. Remove the tofu from the pan and set aside.
3. In the same pan, add a little more oil if needed and sauté the sliced or diced vegetables until they are tender yet still slightly crisp.
4. In a small bowl, mix together doenjang, soy sauce, sesame oil, and minced garlic to create the sauce.
5. Add the cooked tofu back into the pan, followed by the sauce mixture.
6. Stir-fry everything together until the tofu and vegetables are well coated with the sauce and the flavors are well combined.
7. Remove from heat and garnish with sliced green onions and sesame seeds, if desired.
8. Serve the Doenjang Tofu Stir-Fry hot with steamed rice or as a filling for lettuce wraps for a delightful and satisfying vegan dish.

Enjoy the delightful flavors of Doenjang Bibimbap, Doenjang Japchae, and Doenjang Tofu Stir-Fry as you explore the versatility of doenjang in vegetarian and vegan cuisine. These recipes offer a range of textures and tastes, combining the rich umami flavor of doenjang with an array of colorful vegetables and plant-based ingredients. So, embrace the world of plant-based goodness and savor the deliciousness of these vegetarian and vegan dishes enhanced by the unique taste of doenjang.

Chapter 12: Doenjang Desserts and Sweets

In this chapter, we will venture into the realm of sweet treats and desserts featuring the unexpected ingredient of doenjang. These recipes showcase the versatility of doenjang by incorporating it into delectable desserts that will surprise and delight your taste buds. Get ready to indulge in the unique flavors of Doenjang Brownies, Doenjang Ice Cream, and Doenjang Rice Cake (Tteok) Balls.

a. Doenjang Brownies

Doenjang Brownies are a creative twist on the classic chocolate treat, adding a subtle depth of savory flavor to the rich sweetness. These brownies are perfect for those who enjoy the combination of sweet and savory elements. Here's how you can prepare these unique and indulgent brownies:

Ingredients:

- 1 cup all-purpose flour
- 1/2 cup unsweetened cocoa powder
- 1/2 teaspoon baking powder
- 1/4 teaspoon salt
- 1/2 cup unsalted butter, melted
- 1 cup granulated sugar
- 2 large eggs
- 2 teaspoons vanilla extract
- 2 tablespoons doenjang (Korean soybean paste)
- Optional: Chopped nuts or chocolate chips for added texture

Instructions:

1. Preheat the oven to 350°F (175°C) and grease a square baking pan.
2. In a mixing bowl, whisk together the flour, cocoa powder, baking powder, and salt.
3. In a separate large bowl, combine the melted butter, sugar, eggs, and vanilla extract. Mix well until the sugar is dissolved and the mixture is smooth.
4. Gradually add the dry ingredients to the wet ingredients, stirring until just combined. Be careful not to overmix.
5. Gently fold in the doenjang until it is evenly incorporated into the batter.
6. If desired, fold in chopped nuts or chocolate chips.
7. Pour the batter into the greased baking pan and spread it evenly.
8. Bake in the preheated oven for approximately 25-30 minutes or until a toothpick inserted into the center comes out with a few moist crumbs.
9. Remove from the oven and let the brownies cool in the pan before cutting into squares.
10. Serve the Doenjang Brownies as a unique and flavorful dessert, and enjoy the intriguing combination of sweet chocolate and savory doenjang.

b. Doenjang Ice Cream

Doenjang Ice Cream offers a surprising and delightful twist on a frozen treat. The addition of doenjang creates a unique umami undertone that pairs beautifully with the creamy and sweet flavors of traditional ice cream. Here's how you can make this intriguing ice cream:

Ingredients:

- 2 cups heavy cream
- 1 cup whole milk
- 3/4 cup granulated sugar
- 4 large egg yolks
- 2 teaspoons vanilla extract
- 2 tablespoons doenjang (Korean soybean paste)

Instructions:

1. In a saucepan, combine the heavy cream and whole milk. Heat the mixture over medium heat until it reaches a gentle simmer. Remove from heat.
2. In a mixing bowl, whisk together the sugar and egg yolks until they are well combined and slightly thickened.
3. Gradually pour the hot cream mixture into the bowl with the sugar and egg yolks, whisking constantly to prevent curdling.
4. Return the mixture to the saucepan and place it back over medium heat. Cook, stirring constantly, until the mixture thickens and coats the back of a spoon. This should take about 5-7 minutes. Do not let it come to a boil.
5. Remove from heat and stir in the vanilla extract.
6. In a separate bowl, whisk the doenjang until it becomes smooth and creamy.
7. Add the doenjang to the hot ice cream base, whisking until it is fully incorporated.
8. Allow the mixture to cool to room temperature, then cover and

refrigerate for at least 4 hours or overnight to chill completely.

9. Once chilled, pour the mixture into an ice cream maker and churn according to the manufacturer's instructions.

10. Transfer the churned ice cream to a lidded container and freeze for an additional 2-3 hours to firm up.

11. Serve the Doenjang Ice Cream in bowls or cones, and enjoy the surprising combination of creamy sweetness and subtle savory notes.

c. Doenjang Rice Cake (Tteok) Balls

Doenjang Rice Cake (Tteok) Balls offer a unique twist on the traditional Korean rice cake, incorporating the savory flavors of doenjang into a delightful bite-sized treat. These balls are perfect for snacking or as a dessert option. Here's how you can make these flavorful and chewy tteok balls:

Ingredients:

- 2 cups glutinous rice flour
- 2 tablespoons doenjang (Korean soybean paste)
- 1 tablespoon honey or maple syrup
- 1 cup hot water
- Optional coatings: Ground sesame seeds, chopped nuts, or cocoa powder

Instructions:

1. In a mixing bowl, combine the glutinous rice flour, doenjang, and honey (or maple syrup).
2. Gradually add the hot water to the bowl, stirring continuously, until a smooth and sticky dough forms. Adjust the amount of water as needed to achieve the right consistency.
3. Once the dough is well mixed, allow it to rest for about 10 minutes to firm up slightly.
4. Divide the dough into small portions and roll them into bite-sized balls.
5. If desired, roll the balls in ground sesame seeds, chopped nuts, or cocoa powder for added texture and flavor.
6. Place the tteok balls on a plate or tray lined with parchment paper to prevent sticking.
7. Let the tteok balls cool and set at room temperature for about 15-20 minutes.
8. Serve the Doenjang Rice Cake (Tteok) Balls as a unique and

satisfying dessert or snack option, and enjoy the chewy texture and savory-sweet flavors.

Indulge in the surprising and delightful world of Doenjang Brownies, Doenjang Ice Cream, and Doenjang Rice Cake (Tteok) Balls as you explore the unique incorporation of doenjang into desserts and sweets. These recipes showcase the versatility of doenjang by infusing it into unexpected treats, offering a fascinating blend of sweet and savory flavors. So, treat yourself to these intriguing creations and satisfy your sweet tooth with a touch of doenjang's distinctive taste.

Chapter 13: Doenjang and Fermented Foods

In this chapter, we will delve into the world of fermented foods and explore how doenjang can enhance the flavors and benefits of these culinary delights. Fermentation brings a unique tanginess and complexity to ingredients, and when combined with doenjang, it creates a harmonious blend of flavors. Get ready to discover the wonders of Doenjang Kimchi, Doenjang Pickles, and Doenjang Fermented Vegetables.

a. Doenjang Kimchi

Doenjang Kimchi is a delightful variation of the beloved Korean staple, combining the traditional fermentation process of kimchi with the savory depth of doenjang. This fusion kimchi offers a rich umami flavor that complements the spicy and tangy notes of traditional kimchi. Here's how you can prepare this unique and flavorful fermented dish:

Ingredients:

- 1 napa cabbage, cut into bite-sized pieces
- 1/4 cup doenjang (Korean soybean paste)
- 2 tablespoons gochugaru (Korean red pepper flakes)
- 1 tablespoon grated ginger
- 2 cloves of garlic, minced
- 1 tablespoon fish sauce or soy sauce for a vegan option
- 1 tablespoon sugar
- Optional: Sliced green onions and sesame seeds for garnish

Instructions:

1. In a large bowl, combine doenjang, gochugaru, grated ginger,

minced garlic, fish sauce (or soy sauce), and sugar. Mix well to create a smooth paste.

2. Add the napa cabbage to the bowl and thoroughly coat it with the doenjang paste, ensuring that every piece is evenly coated.

3. Transfer the coated cabbage to a fermentation jar or airtight container, pressing down firmly to remove any air pockets.

4. Leave the jar at room temperature for 1-2 days to allow the kimchi to ferment. During this time, open the jar occasionally to release any built-up gases.

5. After the initial fermentation period, transfer the jar to the refrigerator to slow down the fermentation process and allow the flavors to develop further.

6. Let the Doenjang Kimchi ferment in the refrigerator for at least 1 week before consuming to fully develop its flavors.

7. Serve the Doenjang Kimchi as a side dish or condiment to add a delightful tangy and savory kick to your meals. Garnish with sliced green onions and sesame seeds, if desired.

b. Doenjang Pickles

Doenjang Pickles are a unique twist on traditional pickled vegetables, infusing them with the rich and savory flavors of doenjang. These pickles offer a tangy and crunchy experience with a delightful umami undertone. Here's how you can prepare these delicious and versatile pickles:

Ingredients:

- Assorted vegetables of your choice (such as cucumbers, radishes, carrots, and bell peppers), sliced or cut into sticks
- 1/4 cup doenjang (Korean soybean paste)
- 2 tablespoons rice vinegar or apple cider vinegar
- 1 tablespoon sugar
- 1 teaspoon salt
- Optional: Sliced chili peppers or garlic cloves for added flavor

Instructions:

1. In a bowl, mix together doenjang, rice vinegar (or apple cider vinegar), sugar, and salt until well combined.
2. Place the sliced or cut vegetables in a clean glass jar or container.
3. Pour the doenjang mixture over the vegetables, ensuring that they are fully coated.
4. Add sliced chili peppers or garlic cloves, if desired, for additional flavor.
5. Tightly seal the jar or container and let it sit at room temperature for 1-2 days to initiate the fermentation process.
6. After the initial fermentation period, transfer the jar to the refrigerator to slow down the fermentation and allow the flavors to develop further.
7. Let the Doenjang Pickles ferment in the refrigerator for at least 1 week before consuming to fully develop their flavors.
8. Serve the Doenjang Pickles as a tangy and crunchy side dish or

as a flavorful addition to sandwiches, wraps, or salads.

c. Doenjang Fermented Vegetables

Doenjang Fermented Vegetables offer a versatile and delicious way to incorporate the benefits of fermentation and the savory taste of doenjang into a medley of vegetables. This recipe allows you to create your own combination of fermented vegetables based on your preferences. Here's a general guide on how to prepare these delightful fermented veggies:

Ingredients:

- Assorted vegetables of your choice (such as cabbage, radishes, carrots, onions, and peppers), cut into desired shapes
- 1/4 cup doenjang (Korean soybean paste)
- 1 tablespoon salt
- 1 tablespoon sugar
- Optional: Grated ginger, minced garlic, or chili flakes for added flavor

Instructions:

1. In a large bowl, combine doenjang, salt, sugar, and any optional ingredients you prefer, such as grated ginger, minced garlic, or chili flakes. Mix well to create a smooth paste.
2. Add the assorted vegetables to the bowl and thoroughly coat them with the doenjang paste, ensuring that every piece is evenly coated.
3. Transfer the coated vegetables to a fermentation jar or airtight container, pressing down firmly to remove any air pockets.
4. Leave the jar at room temperature for 1-2 days to initiate the fermentation process. Remember to open the jar occasionally to release any built-up gases.
5. After the initial fermentation period, transfer the jar to the refrigerator to slow down the fermentation process and allow

the flavors to develop further.

6. Let the Doenjang Fermented Vegetables ferment in the refrigerator for at least 1 week before consuming to fully develop their flavors.

7. Serve the Doenjang Fermented Vegetables as a tasty and nutritious side dish or incorporate them into your favorite recipes for added depth of flavor.

Enjoy the exciting flavors and benefits of fermented foods with the addition of doenjang in Doenjang Kimchi, Doenjang Pickles, and Doenjang Fermented Vegetables. These recipes offer a unique twist on traditional fermented dishes, infusing them with the savory richness of doenjang. So, embark on a flavorful journey of fermentation and indulge in the tangy and umami delights of these fermented creations.

Chapter 14: Doenjang Beverages

In this chapter, we will explore the unexpected yet intriguing use of doenjang in beverages. While traditionally known as a savory ingredient, doenjang can add a unique and complex flavor profile to drinks, resulting in delightful and inventive beverages. Get ready to discover the world of Doenjang Smoothie, Doenjang Latte, and Doenjang Cocktail.

a. Doenjang Smoothie

Doenjang Smoothie is a surprising and nutritious drink that combines the savory taste of doenjang with a blend of fruits and other ingredients. This smoothie offers a balance of flavors and a hint of umami, making it a refreshing and satisfying beverage. Here's how you can prepare this unconventional smoothie:

Ingredients:

- 1 cup mixed fruits of your choice (such as berries, banana, mango, or pineapple)
- 1 cup unsweetened almond milk or your preferred milk alternative
- 2 tablespoons doenjang (Korean soybean paste)
- 1 tablespoon honey or maple syrup
- Optional: Ice cubes for a chilled smoothie

Instructions:

1. In a blender, combine the mixed fruits, almond milk (or milk alternative), doenjang, and honey (or maple syrup).
2. Blend on high speed until all the ingredients are well combined and the smoothie reaches a creamy consistency.
3. If desired, add ice cubes to the blender and blend again to create

a chilled smoothie.

4. Pour the Doenjang Smoothie into a glass and serve it immediately as a nutritious and unexpected beverage option.

b. Doenjang Latte

Doenjang Latte is a comforting and unique twist on a traditional latte, incorporating the savory notes of doenjang into a warm and frothy drink. This beverage offers a delightful combination of flavors, perfect for cozy mornings or relaxing evenings. Here's how you can prepare this intriguing latte:

Ingredients:

- 1 cup milk of your choice
- 1 tablespoon doenjang (Korean soybean paste)
- 1 teaspoon honey or your preferred sweetener
- Optional: Pinch of cinnamon or nutmeg for added flavor

Instructions:

1. In a small saucepan, heat the milk over medium-low heat until it becomes warm but not boiling.
2. In a separate bowl, whisk together doenjang and honey (or your preferred sweetener) until they are well combined and the doenjang is dissolved.
3. Pour the warm milk into the bowl with the doenjang mixture, whisking continuously to create a smooth and frothy latte.
4. If desired, add a pinch of cinnamon or nutmeg to enhance the flavor of the latte.
5. Pour the Doenjang Latte into a mug and serve it hot, enjoying the comforting and savory notes of this unique beverage.

c. Doenjang Cocktail

Doenjang Cocktail is a creative and adventurous drink that combines the savory richness of doenjang with other ingredients to create a complex and intriguing cocktail experience. This beverage is perfect for those who enjoy experimenting with flavors and pushing the boundaries of traditional mixology. Here's how you can prepare this bold and unconventional cocktail:

Ingredients:

- 2 ounces soju or vodka
- 1 tablespoon doenjang (Korean soybean paste)
- 1/2 ounce lemon juice
- 1/2 ounce simple syrup
- Ice cubes
- Optional: Sliced cucumber or mint leaves for garnish

Instructions:

1. In a cocktail shaker, combine soju (or vodka), doenjang, lemon juice, and simple syrup.

2. Add a few ice cubes to the shaker and shake vigorously for about 20-30 seconds to thoroughly mix the ingredients and chill the cocktail.
3. Strain the Doenjang Cocktail into a glass filled with ice cubes.
4. If desired, garnish with a slice of cucumber or a few mint leaves for a refreshing touch.
5. Serve the Doenjang Cocktail and enjoy the intriguing combination of savory doenjang with the other flavors in this adventurous beverage.

Embark on a unique taste adventure with Doenjang Smoothie, Doenjang Latte, and Doenjang Cocktail. These beverages showcase the versatility of doenjang by infusing it into unexpected drink options, creating intriguing flavor profiles. So, let your taste buds explore the boundaries of traditional beverages and savor the delightful and inventive flavors of these Doenjang-inspired drinks.

Chapter 15: Doenjang for Special Occasions

In this chapter, we will explore the use of doenjang in special occasion dishes that are perfect for gatherings and celebrations. These recipes highlight the rich and savory flavors of doenjang while creating memorable culinary experiences. Get ready to impress your guests with Doenjang Jeon (Korean Pancakes), Doenjang Mandu (Dumplings), and Doenjang BBQ Feast.

a. Doenjang Jeon (Korean Pancakes)

Doenjang Jeon, also known as Korean Pancakes, are a popular dish that combines the crispy texture of pancakes with the savory taste of doenjang. These pancakes are a delightful addition to special occasions, serving as appetizers or side dishes. Here's how you can prepare this delicious and crowd-pleasing dish:

Ingredients:

- 1 cup all-purpose flour
- 1 cup water
- 2 tablespoons doenjang (Korean soybean paste)
- 1 small onion, thinly sliced
- 1 small zucchini, thinly sliced
- 4-5 green onions, chopped
- Vegetable oil for frying
- Optional dipping sauce: Soy sauce, vinegar, and sesame oil mixture

Instructions:

1. In a mixing bowl, whisk together flour, water, and doenjang

until the batter is smooth and well combined.

2. Add the sliced onion, zucchini, and chopped green onions to the batter. Mix well to ensure the vegetables are evenly coated.

3. Heat a large non-stick pan or skillet over medium heat and add a thin layer of vegetable oil.

4. Spoon the batter onto the pan, using about 1/4 to 1/3 cup of batter per pancake, depending on your desired size.

5. Flatten and spread the batter with the back of a spoon to form round pancakes.

6. Cook the pancakes for about 2-3 minutes on each side, or until they turn golden brown and crispy.

7. Transfer the cooked pancakes to a serving plate lined with paper towels to absorb any excess oil.

8. Repeat the process with the remaining batter and vegetables until all the pancakes are cooked.

9. Serve the Doenjang Jeon hot as appetizers or side dishes. For added flavor, dip the pancakes in a mixture of soy sauce, vinegar, and sesame oil.

b. Doenjang Mandu (Dumplings)

Doenjang Mandu, or Doenjang Dumplings, are delightful bite-sized treats filled with a savory mixture and enhanced by the rich taste of doenjang. These dumplings make a great addition to special occasions, whether steamed, boiled, or pan-fried. Here's how you can prepare these flavorful and festive dumplings:

Ingredients:

- 1 package dumpling wrappers (round or square)
- 1 cup ground pork or tofu for a vegetarian option
- 1/2 cup doenjang (Korean soybean paste)
- 1/4 cup finely chopped cabbage
- 1/4 cup minced onion
- 1/4 cup minced green onions
- 2 cloves of garlic, minced
- 1 tablespoon sesame oil
- Optional: Finely chopped vegetables or mushrooms for added texture and flavor
- Optional dipping sauce: Soy sauce, vinegar, sesame oil, and a pinch of sugar

Instructions:

1. In a mixing bowl, combine ground pork (or tofu), doenjang, chopped cabbage, minced onion, minced green onions, minced garlic, sesame oil, and any optional ingredients you prefer. Mix well until all the ingredients are thoroughly incorporated.
2. Place a small spoonful of the filling mixture in the center of a dumpling wrapper.
3. Moisten the edges of the wrapper with water and fold it in half, sealing the edges tightly to form a half-moon shape. You can create pleats along the edges for an added decorative touch.
4. Repeat the process with the remaining filling and wrappers until

all the dumplings are assembled.

5. To cook the dumplings, you have several options: steaming, boiling, or pan-frying.

6. Steaming: Place the dumplings in a steamer basket and steam them over boiling water for about 10-12 minutes, or until they are cooked through.

7. Boiling: Bring a pot of water to a boil and carefully add the dumplings. Cook for about 6-8 minutes, or until they float to the surface and are cooked through.

8. Pan-frying: Heat a non-stick pan over medium heat and add a small amount of oil. Place the dumplings in the pan and cook for a few minutes until the bottoms are golden brown. Then, add water to the pan, cover, and cook for an additional 6-8 minutes, or until the dumplings are cooked through.

9. Once cooked, serve the Doenjang Mandu hot as a delightful appetizer or main dish. For dipping, prepare a sauce by combining soy sauce, vinegar, sesame oil, and a pinch of sugar.

c. Doenjang BBQ Feast

Doenjang BBQ Feast is a grand spread of grilled meats and vegetables marinated in a savory doenjang sauce. This feast is perfect for special occasions, bringing together the smoky flavors of the grill with the rich umami taste of doenjang. Here's how you can create a memorable Doenjang BBQ Feast:

Ingredients:

- Assorted meats such as beef, pork, chicken, or seafood
- Assorted vegetables such as mushrooms, bell peppers, zucchini, onions, or eggplant
- For the doenjang marinade:
- 1/4 cup doenjang (Korean soybean paste)
- 2 tablespoons soy sauce
- 2 tablespoons honey or brown sugar
- 2 tablespoons sesame oil
- 2 cloves of garlic, minced
- 1 tablespoon grated ginger
- Optional: Chili flakes or sliced chili peppers for spice

Instructions:

1. In a mixing bowl, combine doenjang, soy sauce, honey (or brown sugar), sesame oil, minced garlic, grated ginger, and any optional ingredients for spice. Mix well until the marinade is smooth and well combined.
2. Marinate the meats and vegetables in the doenjang marinade for at least 1 hour or overnight in the refrigerator, allowing the flavors to infuse.
3. Preheat a grill or grill pan to medium-high heat.
4. Grill the marinated meats and vegetables until they are cooked to your desired level of doneness, basting them with the remaining marinade for added flavor.

5. Remove the grilled items from the heat and arrange them on a serving platter.
6. Serve the Doenjang BBQ Feast as a centerpiece for your special occasion, allowing your guests to enjoy the grilled meats and vegetables with the rich and savory flavors of doenjang.

Impress your guests with the delightful flavors of Doenjang Jeon, Doenjang Mandu, and Doenjang BBQ Feast. These recipes bring a touch of Korean culinary tradition to your special occasions, incorporating the savory depth of doenjang into memorable dishes that are sure to be a hit. So, gather your loved ones, celebrate, and savor the deliciousness of these special occasion treats enhanced by the unique taste of doenjang.

Chapter 16: Doenjang Health Benefits and Nutritional Information

In this chapter, we will explore the health benefits and nutritional information of doenjang, highlighting its potential positive impact on your well-being. Doenjang not only adds a unique flavor to dishes but also offers several nutritional advantages. Let's dive into the health benefits and nutritional profile of this traditional Korean soybean paste.

Health Benefits of Doenjang:

Rich in Protein: Doenjang is a significant source of plant-based protein, making it a valuable addition to vegetarian and vegan diets. Protein is essential for various bodily functions, including tissue repair and the production of enzymes and hormones.

Probiotic Properties: Doenjang is a fermented food, which means it contains beneficial bacteria that support gut health. These probiotics help promote a healthy digestive system and contribute to improved overall digestion and nutrient absorption.

Source of Essential Amino Acids: Doenjang contains essential amino acids, which are the building blocks of proteins that the body cannot produce on its own. Consuming foods rich in essential amino acids is important for maintaining optimal health and supporting various bodily functions.

Antioxidant Activity: Fermented foods like doenjang are known to possess antioxidant properties. Antioxidants help protect the body against oxidative stress and damage caused by free radicals, reducing the risk of chronic diseases and supporting overall well-being.

Potential Blood Pressure Regulation: Studies suggest that the consumption of fermented soy products, including doenjang, may have a positive impact on blood pressure regulation. The presence of bioactive compounds in doenjang may contribute to these beneficial effects.

Nutritional Information of Doenjang (per 1 tablespoon serving):

Calories: 40

Total Fat: 1.5g

Saturated Fat: 0g

Trans Fat: 0g

Cholesterol: 0mg

Sodium: 730mg

Total Carbohydrate: 3g

Dietary Fiber: 1g

Sugars: 1g

Protein: 4g

Vitamin K: 20% of the Recommended Daily Intake (RDI)

Iron: 6% of the RDI

Note: The nutritional information may vary slightly depending on the brand and specific recipe of doenjang used.

It's important to note that while doenjang offers various health benefits, its high sodium content should be considered for individuals who need to monitor their sodium intake, such as those with high blood pressure or certain health conditions. Moderation and balance are key when incorporating doenjang into your diet.

By incorporating doenjang into your meals, you can enjoy not only its unique flavor but also its potential health benefits. From its protein content to probiotic properties and antioxidant activity, doenjang offers a range of advantages that contribute to overall well-being. Remember to consume doenjang as part of a balanced diet and consult with a healthcare professional or nutritionist for personalized dietary advice.

Chapter 17: Tips and Techniques for Cooking with Doenjang

In this chapter, we will explore some valuable tips and techniques to enhance your cooking experience with doenjang. Whether you're a seasoned cook or just starting to experiment with this traditional Korean ingredient, these tips will help you make the most of doenjang's unique flavor and incorporate it into a variety of dishes. Let's dive in!

Start with Small Amounts: Doenjang has a robust and concentrated flavor, so it's best to start with small amounts and gradually increase as per your taste preferences. A little goes a long way in adding depth and umami to your dishes.

Mix Well for Smooth Texture: Doenjang can have a thick and grainy texture, especially when directly added to a dish. To ensure a smooth texture and even distribution, it's recommended to mix doenjang with a small amount of liquid (water, broth, or sauce) until it becomes a smooth paste before adding it to your recipes.

Experiment with Different Types of Doenjang: There are different varieties of doenjang available, such as regular doenjang, aged doenjang, and white doenjang. Each type may have slight flavor variations, so feel free to experiment and find your favorite type for different dishes.

Balance with Other Flavors: Doenjang has a rich, savory taste that pairs well with other ingredients. Balance its flavor by incorporating sweet, sour, or spicy elements in your dish. For example, you can add a touch of sweetness with honey or balance it with vinegar or citrus juice.

Use in Soups, Stews, and Marinades: Doenjang is a versatile ingredient that can be used in various dishes. It shines particularly well in soups and stews, adding depth and complexity to the broth. It also works wonderfully as a base for marinades, imparting a savory and umami flavor to meats and vegetables.

Incorporate in Stir-Fries and Sauteed Dishes: Add doenjang to stir-fries and sauteed dishes to elevate their taste. It adds a savory punch and works beautifully with vegetables, meats, or tofu. Sauté your ingredients with a small amount of doenjang for a deliciously seasoned outcome.

Enjoy as a Dipping Sauce: Mix doenjang with other ingredients like sesame oil, soy sauce, garlic, and vinegar to create a flavorful dipping sauce. It pairs well with grilled meats, vegetables, or even as a condiment for dumplings or pancakes.

Store Properly: Doenjang is a fermented product, and proper storage is essential to maintain its quality. Keep it in an airtight container in the refrigerator, and ensure the lid is tightly closed to prevent air exposure. Proper storage will help preserve its flavor and prevent spoilage.

Explore Fusion Cuisine: Don't be afraid to think outside the box and incorporate doenjang into non-traditional dishes. It can add a unique twist to fusion cuisine like pasta, pizza, or even salad dressings. Let your creativity guide you and enjoy the unexpected flavor combinations.

Adjust Other Seasonings: Since doenjang has a distinct flavor, you may need to adjust other seasonings in your recipe accordingly. Taste and adjust the salt, soy sauce, or other seasonings to achieve a well-balanced dish.

Remember, cooking with doenjang is a culinary adventure that allows you to explore and experiment with unique flavors. These tips and techniques will help you make the most of this traditional Korean ingredient, enhancing the taste of your dishes and expanding your culinary repertoire. So, embrace the versatility of doenjang and let it take your cooking to new heights!

Chapter 18: Exploring Different Varieties of Doenjang

In this chapter, we will delve into the world of different varieties of doenjang, each offering its own unique flavors and characteristics. While the traditional doenjang is widely known and loved, there are other variations that can add depth and complexity to your dishes. Let's explore and discover the diverse flavors of different types of doenjang.

Traditional Doenjang: Traditional doenjang, also known as "jangdoenjang," is the most common and widely available variety. It is made from fermented soybeans, salt, and sometimes other ingredients like rice or barley. Traditional doenjang has a rich, savory taste with deep umami flavors. It is typically aged for several months or even years, resulting in a more complex and robust flavor profile.

Aged Doenjang: Aged doenjang, also referred to as "jangjangdoenjang," undergoes a longer fermentation process, often for one to three years or more. This extended aging process enhances the flavors and intensifies the umami characteristics of the doenjang. Aged doenjang offers a more pronounced and nuanced taste, making it ideal for dishes where a stronger flavor is desired.

White Doenjang: White doenjang, or "haedoekdoenjang," is a variety of doenjang that is made with soybeans but without the soybean hulls. The removal of the hulls results in a lighter-colored paste with a milder and slightly sweeter taste compared to traditional doenjang. White doenjang is often preferred for dishes that require a more delicate flavor or for those who prefer a milder taste.

Quick-Fermented Doenjang: Quick-fermented doenjang, also known as "sseolmaedoekdoenjang," is a variety that undergoes a shorter fermentation process. It is typically fermented for a few weeks to a few months, resulting in a milder and fresher flavor compared to traditional doenjang. Quick-fermented doenjang is a good option for those who prefer a less intense taste or for dishes where a lighter flavor is desired.

Homemade Doenjang: Making your own doenjang at home allows you to experiment and create a personalized version of this traditional Korean paste. Homemade doenjang can be customized based on your preferences, allowing you to control the fermentation time, ingredients, and flavors. It offers a rewarding experience and a unique taste that can't be replicated with store-bought varieties.

When exploring different varieties of doenjang, it's important to consider your personal taste preferences and the specific dish you are preparing. Each type of doenjang brings its own distinct flavor profile to your culinary creations, enhancing the overall taste experience. Whether you opt for the traditional, aged, white, quick-fermented, or homemade variety, the key is to experiment, discover your favorites, and enjoy the diverse range of flavors that doenjang has to offer.

Remember to store doenjang properly according to the specific instructions provided for each variety to maintain its quality and flavor. With a variety of doenjang options at your disposal, you can elevate your dishes, experiment with different flavor profiles, and embark on a delicious journey through the world of doenjang.

Chapter 19: Doenjang Pairings and Menu Suggestions

In this chapter, we will explore some delicious pairings and menu suggestions to help you create well-balanced and flavorful meals using doenjang. Whether you're looking to incorporate doenjang into traditional Korean dishes or explore fusion cuisine, these suggestions will inspire you to create exciting and satisfying menus. Let's dive in!

Traditional Korean Menu:

Main Dish: Doenjang Jjigae (Doenjang Stew) served with steamed rice.
Side Dish 1: Kongnamul Muchim (Seasoned Soybean Sprouts).
Side Dish 2: Oi Doenjang Muchim (Cucumber Doenjang Salad).
Side Dish 3: Doenjang Jeon (Korean Pancakes).
Dessert: Doenjang Rice Cake (Tteok) Balls.

BBQ Feast Menu:

Main Dish: Doenjang Marinated Grilled Beef (Doenjang Bulgogi) served with grilled vegetables like mushrooms, bell peppers, and onions.
Side Dish 1: Doenjang Kimchi.
Side Dish 2: Gamja Doenjang Bokkeum (Stir-Fried Potatoes with Doenjang).
Side Dish 3: Doenjang Pickles.
Beverage: Doenjang Cocktail for a unique and flavorful drink option.

Fusion Cuisine Menu:

Main Dish: Doenjang Fried Rice with your choice of protein like chicken, shrimp, or tofu.
Appetizer: Doenjang Mandu (Dumplings) served with a dipping sauce.

Side Dish 1: Doenjang Pasta with sautéed vegetables and grated Parmesan cheese.

Side Dish 2: Doenjang Glazed Tofu served with a side of mixed greens.

Dessert: Doenjang Brownies for a surprising and indulgent sweet treat.

Vegetarian/Vegan Menu:

Main Dish: Doenjang Bibimbap (Mixed Rice Bowl) with assorted vegetables, tofu, and a fried egg or a vegan egg substitute.

Side Dish 1: Doenjang Japchae (Stir-Fried Glass Noodles with Vegetables).

Side Dish 2: Doenjang Tofu Stir-Fry with broccoli, bell peppers, and snow peas.

Side Dish 3: Assorted Doenjang Fermented Vegetables.

Beverage: Doenjang Smoothie with mixed fruits and almond milk.

Seafood Delights Menu:

Main Dish: Doenjang Jjigae with Clams, featuring a flavorful combination of doenjang stew and fresh clams.

Side Dish 1: Grilled Doenjang Shrimp Skewers marinated in a doenjang-based glaze.

Side Dish 2: Spicy Doenjang Steamed Fish, steamed to perfection with a spicy doenjang sauce.

Side Dish 3: Doenjang Ramyeon (Doenjang Instant Noodles) with added seafood like shrimp or mussels.

Dessert: Doenjang Ice Cream for a unique and refreshing sweet ending.

Remember, these menu suggestions are just a starting point, and you can mix and match dishes according to your preferences and dietary needs. Don't hesitate to experiment and create your own combinations using doenjang as the star ingredient. Whether you're planning a traditional Korean feast, exploring fusion cuisine, or catering to specific dietary requirements, doenjang adds a savory and unique touch to your menu, taking your culinary creations to new heights of flavor and satisfaction.

In this cookbook, we have explored the wonderful world of Doenjang, the traditional Korean soybean paste. From its rich history and significance in Korean cuisine to its health benefits, we have delved into the many aspects that make Doenjang a versatile and exciting ingredient to work with in the kitchen.

Throughout the chapters, we have provided you with a variety of recipes, tips, techniques, and menu suggestions to inspire your culinary adventures with Doenjang. Whether you're a fan of traditional Korean dishes, a lover of fusion cuisine, or simply looking to add depth and umami to your meals, Doenjang has proven to be a fantastic addition to a wide range of recipes.

From classic Doenjang stews and soups to creative fusion dishes, Doenjang has shown its ability to elevate flavors and create memorable dining experiences. The homemade Doenjang guide has empowered you to craft your own batch of this traditional paste, giving you the opportunity to experiment and personalize the flavors to your liking.

We have discussed the health benefits and nutritional information of Doenjang, highlighting its protein content, probiotic properties, and antioxidant activity. It is important to remember that moderation and balance are key when incorporating Doenjang into your diet, especially considering its sodium content.

With each chapter, we aimed to provide you with clear and concise information, guiding you step by step through the recipes, techniques, and suggestions. We hope this cookbook has inspired you to explore the diverse and delicious possibilities of Doenjang and encouraged you to embrace its unique flavor in your cooking.

So, whether you're preparing a traditional Korean feast, hosting a BBQ gathering, experimenting with fusion dishes, or seeking vegetarian and vegan options, Doenjang can be your trusted companion, adding depth, complexity, and a touch of Korean tradition to your culinary creations.

Now it's time for you to dive into the world of Doenjang, get creative in the kitchen, and savor the delightful flavors and experiences that this remarkable ingredient has to offer. Happy cooking!